My Prayer Journal

by Mary J. Davis

LEGACY PRESS
A Division of Rainbow Publishers

My Prayer Journal
©2001 by Legacy Press, fifth printing
ISBN 1-885358-37-7
DB46731

Legacy Press
P.O. Box 261129
San Diego, CA 92196

Illustrator: Joel Ryan
Editor: Christy Allen
Cover Design: Stray Cat Studio, San Diego, CA

Unless otherwise noted, scriptures are from the
Holy Bible: New International Version (North
American edition), ©1973, 1978, 1984 by the
International Bible Society. Used by permission
of Zondervan Bible Publishers.

Printed in the United States of America

Table of Contents

Introduction 5

A New Adventure 7

Getting to Know God 23

Living God's Way...41

Loving Others 55

This Thing Called Life 81

Praising God 97

Uncontrollable Monsters! 111

A Gratitude Attitude 129

In Conclusion 143

Introduction

Do you sometimes wish for a special friend who understands what you are going through? Are there times when you are so filled with joy that you could burst, or so full of sorrow that you don't know where to turn?

No matter what is going on in your life, God is waiting to hear from you. He longs to share your joys, sorrows, fears, and whatever else may come your way each and every day. This journal will help you to have a wonderful prayer life and to become closer to God. You will begin to realize that God is your best friend and that you can share any secret with Him.

Each part of this journal is designed to help you build a strong prayer life and to take every opportunity to worship our great and caring God.

To make the best use of your prayer journal, follow these steps:

Think About This

Read the thought and consider how it relates to your life. Does this ever happen to you? How do you feel about this? How can God help you?

What God's Word Says

Isn't it amazing that God has an answer for every question and problem we might have? Look up the scripture in your own Bible. Read it to yourself. Then read it aloud to God. Ask God to help you know how His Word will help you this week.

My Prayer Requests

This space is for you to write out anything you want to tell God.

God Works It out

You may use this spot in two different ways. You may come back to this page later, when you feel that God has answered your prayer, and write down how He answered it. This will help you learn how God works constantly in your life. Or, you may write in this spot each day, remembering how God answered other prayers in your life.

Prayer

Read the prayer to yourself and think about how you might ask God to help you in this same kind of situation. Add your own thoughts to the prayer as you say it to God.

Go

You will have an "assignment" each week that will help you learn to put your trust in God and to begin to spread this trust to others who need God's love and care.

There are questions for you to answer at the end of each chapter. These will help you to think back on everything you learned in that chapter.

Enjoy this prayer journal as you learn to tell God everything and trust Him to do what's best in your life. Remember that no problem or need is too great or too small for our wonderful, caring God.

A New Adventure

You often face new situations in your life. While these times are exciting, they can also be a little scary. It's easy to let yourself feel like you are going into a new situation all alone. That makes you even more afraid. But you need to remember that God is always with you. He enters each new area of your life with you.

If you give your fears and worries to God, He will take them upon Himself and give you the strength to face anything. What a wonderful promise!

God is waiting to hear from you. He loves for you to give Him all your worries and trust Him. God wants to hold your hand as you go along life's road.

Instead of entering into a new situation alone, why not share your fears with God in prayer and let Him help you to be strong? This prayer journal is the first of many adventures you will have with God.

✳ Beginnings ✳

Think About This

Today I begin a new adventure, one that will bring me closer to God and help me to become a better Christian. Prayer is a gift from God that allows me to talk to Him and share with Him. When I pray, I am following God's commandment. God is happy when I talk to Him.

What God's Word Says

So I say to you: Ask and it will be given to you; seek and you will find; knock and the door will be opened to you. For everyone who asks receives; he who seeks finds; and to him who knocks, the door will be opened.

— Luke 11:9-10

My Prayer Requests

_____

_____

_____

_____

_____

God Works It Out

_____

_____

_____

Prayer

Thank You, God, that You are always there for me. As I begin this prayer journal, I will try my best to take time each day to talk to You. I know You love to hear from me and that You always have time for me. Amen.

Go

Make a schedule for yourself so you are sure to have time for prayer. Decide which time of day will be best for you to pray. Tell your parents about your decision and ask them to help you to keep your commitment.

✻ Praying Like Jesus ✻

Think About This

I love to read in the Bible where Jesus talked to God. It makes me feel closer to Jesus, knowing that He prayed like I do.

What God's Word Says

Read John, chapter 17. This is Jesus' prayer for Himself to complete God's work, for His disciples to be protected by God while they serve Him, and for all believers, that God's love may be in us, as we serve our Lord.

My Prayer Requests

God Works It Out

_____

_____

_____

Prayer

Pray the Lord's Prayer. It is in Matthew 6:9-13.
Our Father, which art in heaven, hallowed be thy name
Your kingdom come
Your will be done on earth as it is in heaven.
Give us this day our daily bread.
Forgive us our trespasses, as we forgive those who
have trespassed against us.
Lead us not into temptation, but deliver us from evil.
For thine is the kingdom, the power, and the glory.
Amen. (KJV)

Go

Memorize the Lord's Prayer. Ask your parents or
an older brother or sister to help you.

✳ A New School Year ✳

Think About This

This is the beginning of a new school year. The first few days might be a little scary for me. Will I like the new teacher? Will he or she like me? Who will be in my classes that I know?

What God's Word Says

I am with you always, to the very end of the age.
— Matthew 28:20

The Lord watches over all who love him.
— Psalm 145:20

My Prayer Requests

_____

_____

_____

_____

_____

_____

God Works It Out

_____

_____

_____

Prayer

I am afraid to face new classes. Help me get through the first few days, Lord. I will trust You to be with me all of the time. Amen.

Go

When you feel afraid to face new situations, read Psalm 121. Find someone else who is frightened and encourage him or her. You will be surprised how much strength God gives you to help someone else!

✳ Making New Friends ✳

Think About This

I've been with the same group of friends all of my life. Now I have changed schools, or my family has had to move. I need God's help in facing these changes and making new friends.

What God's Word Says

Wait for the Lord; be strong and take heart and wait for the Lord. — Psalm 27:14

My Prayer Requests

_____

_____

_____

_____

_____

_____

God Works It Out

_____

_____

_____

Prayer

All my life I have had the same group of friends. Now I have changed schools, or none of my friends are in my class. Help me to make new friends quickly. If I am not the one who has been taken out of a class with all my friends, maybe I can encourage someone new in my class who needs a friend. Amen.

Go

Make friends with at least one new person this week.

✳ Committing to God ✳

Think About This

I will begin a regular daily time of reading and studying God's Word. I know this will please God.

What God's Word Says

I have hidden your word in my heart that I might not sin against you. — Psalm 119:11

Your word is a lamp unto my feet and a light for my path. — Psalm 119:105

My Prayer Requests

_____

_____

_____

_____

_____

God Works It Out

_____

_____

_____

Prayer

God, help me to begin to read Your Word each day and to understand what You want me to know. James 1:22 tells me to not just listen to Your Word, but to do what it says. I want to follow Your ways. Amen.

Go

Read your Bible for at least 10 minutes each day this week. Did you know there are adventure stories in the Bible? Daniel 3 and 6, the book of Jonah, Psalm 23, the book of Luke and Acts 27 and 28 are all good adventure stories. The Bible also has lots of amazing events (John 11:1-46), romance (the book of Ruth), self-help (the book of James) and comedy (Numbers 22:21-38). Find out why the Bible is the best book ever written!

✳ Serving God ✳

Think About This

Today is a new beginning in serving God. I will serve God in any way that I can. God will help me to find ways to serve Him.

What God's Word Says

Each one should use whatever gift he has received to serve others, faithfully administering God's grace in its various forms.

— 1 Peter 4:10

Therefore go and make disciples of all nations.

— Matthew 28:19

My Prayer Requests

_____

_____

_____

_____

_____

_____

God Works It Out

_____

_____

_____

Prayer

Help me, Lord, to serve You. I know there are some things I can do to help my family, my neighbors or my church. Amen.

Go

Find some way to serve God each day, remembering that even small jobs are serving God, if you do them joyfully.

✳ What I Learned ✳

✳ In this Chapter, I learned:

_____

_____

_____

✳ My favorite Bible verse in this Chapter is:

_____

_____

✳ I was surprised to find out that:

_____

_____

_____

✳ I discovered this about myself:

_____

_____

_____

✳ I discovered this about God:

_____

_____

_____

✳ How I plan to act on what I've learned:

_____

_____

_____

Getting to Know God

Isn't it fun to meet a new friend? There are lots of interesting things to learn about each other. What a blessing it is to have good friends!

We sometimes become such good friends with people that we talk to them almost all of the time on the telephone, meet at the corner to walk to school together, and spend as much time together as we can outside of school. It's especially wonderful to have a friend whom you can trust with your deepest secrets. You could tell your friend anything, and he or she would still be your friend.

Did you know it's possible to be that kind of friend with God? You can have a great time reading the Bible to learn all about Him. You can talk to Him anytime, and all of the time. He can be trusted with your deepest secrets.

The most special thing about becoming good friends with God is that He wants to be a best friend to you as much as you want to with Him. What a great and caring God we have!

✳ The Good Shepherd ✳

Think About This

Who is Jesus? I want to learn all I can about the Savior who laid down His life for me.

What God's Word Says

I am the good shepherd. The good shepherd lays down his life for the sheep.
— John 10:11

I am the good shepherd; I know my sheep and my sheep know me—just as the Father knows me and I know the Father—and I lay down my life for the sheep.
— John 10:14-15

My Prayer Requests

_____

_____

_____

_____

_____

God Works It Out

_____

_____

_____

Prayer

I am glad that I am Your sheep, Jesus. You are the Good Shepherd, and You gave Your life so that I can live in heaven for eternity. Amen.

Go

These scriptures will help you to understand more about what Jesus did for you: Romans 5:8; Isaiah 1:18; and Isaiah 53:6. Read them!

✳ The Resurrection ✳

Think About This

Jesus is the Resurrection! He died for my sins, but God raised Him from the dead. I will live with my Savior in heaven forever.

What God's Word Says

I am the resurrection and the life. He who believes in me will live.

— John 11:25-26

My Prayer Requests

_____

_____

_____

_____

_____

God Works It Out

_____

_____

_____

Prayer

You gave Your life for me, Jesus. Help me to live a life that shows my love for You. Help me to share this wonderful news with others, so that they will know You, too. Amen.

Go

Acts 13:38 and Romans 5:2 are good scriptures for you to memorize. Share them with someone else!

✳ Heaven ✳

Think About This

What is heaven like? Are there really streets of gold there? Will I go there?

What God's Word Says

No eye has seen, no ear has heard, no mind has conceived what God has prepared for those who love him.
— 1 Corinthians 2:9

My Prayer Requests

_____

_____

_____

_____

_____

God Works It Out

_____

_____

_____

Prayer

You are preparing a wonderful place for me to spend eternity with You, Lord. Thank You for being a loving Father. Amen.

Go

Learn more about heaven by reading the book of Revelation in the Bible. Then draw a picture below of what you learned.

✳ faith ✳

Think About This

My pastor talks a lot about "faith." I know I need to remember to have faith in God because He is in control.

What God's Word Says

Now faith is being sure of what we hope for and certain of what we do not see.
— Hebrews 11:1

My Prayer Requests

_____

_____

_____

_____

_____

God Works It Out

_____

_____

_____

Prayer

Lord, having faith in You means that I am sure of Your love and all You have said in the Bible, even though I have never seen You. I know that You are there, and I love You. Amen.

Go

Write out the words of 2 Timothy 1:12 and John 20:31 below. Read them every day this week.

_____

_____

_____

_____

✳ Worthy of Love ✳

Think About This

Are you sure God loves me? I don't feel very lovable some of the time.

What God's Word Says

For he chose us in him before the creation of the world. — Ephesians 1:4

How great is the love the Father has lavished on us, that we should be called children of God! And that is what we are! — 1 John 3:1

My Prayer Requests

_____

_____

_____

_____

_____

God Works It out

_____

_____

_____

Prayer

I feel so unworthy, Lord. Sometimes I don't know why anyone loves me. But then I read about Your great love and know that I am really someone special. Thank You!

Go

Search in your Bible's index for verses that tell you that you are special, loved and needed. The words "love," "salvation" and "children" will help you find some verses. Write them below.

_____

_____

_____

_____

✱ The Best friend ✱

Think About This

My best friend has abandoned me for new friends. I feel left out and hurt. But I know I always have a friend in Jesus, my ultimate best friend.

What God's Word Says

But there is a friend who sticks closer than a brother.
— Proverbs 18:24

My Prayer Requests

_____

_____

_____

_____

_____

God Works It Out

_____

_____

_____

Prayer

Thank You, Lord Jesus, for being a friend who is
<u>always</u> with me. Amen.

Go

Memorize Proverbs 18:24 to help you remember
that you always have a best friend.

✳ The only God ✳

Think About This

There's only one God. No other being is as powerful, wonderful, faithful and loving as my God.

What God's Word Says

For I am God, and there is no other.
— Isaiah 45:22

My Prayer Requests

_____

_____

_____

_____

_____

_____

_____

God Works It Out

_____

_____

_____

Prayer

Sometimes, Lord, I don't serve You or worship You
as I should. I let other things get in the way. Help
me to remember that You are the one and only God,
and that You want to be my friend. Amen.

Go

List below some things that you allow to get in the
way of worshipping God. Then pray for God to help
you push these things aside and worship Him only.

_____

_____

_____

_____

✻ What I Learned ✻

✻ In this chapter, I learned:

_____

_____

_____

✻ My favorite Bible verse in this chapter is:

_____

_____

✻ I was surprised to find out that:

_____

_____

_____

✳ I discovered this about myself:

_____

_____

_____

✳ I discovered this about God:

_____

_____

_____

✳ How I plan to act on what I've learned:

_____

_____

_____

Living God's Way

Boasting, bad language, mean thoughts—these are all things that God hates. He wants you to have good things in your mind so that good actions come from your mind. He is especially proud when you are faithful to Him and to the church, even when others make fun of you.

God expects you to live a clean and pure life. He wants you to fill your mind and heart with godly thoughts. This is His will for you. He is disappointed when you let bad thoughts and unholy ideas take over your mind.

How do you live a life of which God will be proud? You rely on God to help you. You can also fill your mind with Bible study, devote your mouth to prayer and praise, and dedicate yourself to being in church and spending time around other Christians.

Pray each day for God's help in leading a life that pleases Him.

✴ Christian Conduct ✴

Think About This

I will conduct myself like a child of God. I will not boast. I will be especially careful of others' feelings.

What God's Word Says

Let another praise you, and not your own mouth; someone else, and not your own lips. — Proverbs 27:2

My Prayer Requests

_____

_____

_____

_____

_____

_____

God Works It Out

_____

_____

_____

Prayer

Pride in myself is not bad, Lord. But, I know that being overly proud and boastful is not the way You want me to act. Help me to live like "a child of the King." Amen.

Go

Mark 9:35 tells us that Jesus said these words: "If any one wants to be first, he must be the very last, and the servant of all." Find a way this week to put Jesus' words into practice in your life.

✳ Clean Talk ✳

Think About This

I will not use bad language. God wants me to speak with love to His children.

What God's Word Says

May the words of my mouth and the meditation of my heart be pleasing in your sight, O Lord, my Rock and my Redeemer. — Psalm 19:14

My Prayer Requests

_____

_____

_____

_____

_____

_____

God Works It Out

_____

_____

_____

Prayer

Dear Father, please help me to always use language that is pleasing to You. I want others to see Your way for living through my godly actions. Amen.

Go

Memorize Psalm 19:14 to remind you that your words should always be pleasing to God.

✳ Pure Thoughts ✳

Think About This

I will keep bad thoughts from my mind. God wants me to think only about His will.

What God's Word Says

Whatever is true, whatever is noble, whatever is right, whatever is pure, whatever is lovely, whatever is admirable—if anything is excellent or praiseworthy—think about such things. — Philippians 4:8

My Prayer Requests

_____

_____

_____

_____

_____

God Works It Out

_____

_____

_____

Prayer

Help me to think about good things, Lord. If I am around someone who tries to put bad things in my mind, give me the courage to stay away from this person. If it is someone that I must be around, then please fill my mind with good thoughts. Amen.

Go

Practice thinking good thoughts, and stay away from TV shows, movies or music that put ungodly thoughts in your mind. Fill your mind with good things—and chase away bad thoughts.

✳ Standing Strong ✳

Think About This

I will not let it bother me when others make fun of me because I go to church. I will remain faithful to God no matter what is said or done to me.

What God's Word Says

Choose for yourselves this day whom you will serve. But as for me and my household, we will serve the Lord. — Joshua 24:15

My Prayer Requests

_____

_____

_____

_____

_____

God Works It Out

_____

_____

_____

Prayer

Help me to stand strong when my friends make fun of me for worshipping You, Lord. By standing strong, I will be an example to others. Amen.

Go

Memorize Joshua 24:15 to keep in mind when someone teases you about going to church or other Christian activities. Then read Matthew 5:10-12 for strength at those times.

✳ Asking Forgiveness ✳

Think About This

I did something wrong that no one else knows about, even though I said I would conduct myself like a child of God.

What God's Word Says

For God will bring every deed into judgment, including every hidden thing, whether it is good or evil.
— Ecclesiastes 12:14

Everyone who believes in him receives forgiveness of sins through his name.
— Acts 10:43

My Prayer Requests

_____

_____

_____

_____

_____

_____

God Works It Out

_____

_____

_____

Prayer

Heavenly Father, You know everything about me, including the bad things I do. Forgive me for all my sins, even those that no one else knows about. Thank You for being a forgiving and merciful God. Amen.

Go

Ecclesiastes 12:14 is a good scripture to take to heart. When you start to do something that you know is wrong, remember that God knows everything. Always ask yourself first, "Would Jesus do this?"

✳ What I Learned ✳

✳ In this chapter, I learned:

_____

_____

_____

✳ My favorite Bible verse in this chapter is:

_____

_____

✳ I was surprised to find out that:

_____

_____

_____

✳ I discovered this about myself:

_____

_____

_____

✳ I discovered this about God:

_____

_____

_____

✳ How I plan to act on what I've learned:

_____

_____

_____

Loving others

Relationships can be very difficult to handle. Your parents or a brother or sister might be treating you unfairly. Or a friend betrayed you or you betrayed a friend, and you don't know how to regain his or her trust.

Loving others all of the time isn't easy to do. Forgiving is sometimes even more difficult. But, with God's help, you can love and forgive anyone. You can also be the kind of friend who would never gossip about another.

Regular prayer keeps you in tune with God. God wants to help you work out your problems with any type of relationship.

✳ Enemies ✳

Think About This

Why should I love someone who treats me badly? I want to be mean back to them and show them how it feels.

What God's Word Says

Love your enemies and pray for those who persecute you.
— Matthew 5:44

If you love those who love you, what reward will you get?
— Matthew 5:46

And if you greet only your brothers, what are you doing more than others? — Matthew 5:47

My Prayer Requests

_____

_____

_____

_____

_____

_____

God Works It out

_____

_____

_____

Prayer

Loving my enemies isn't easy, Lord. Some people don't treat me very well. If I pray for them and ask for Your help, then I know it will be easier. Wouldn't it be wonderful if I could win at least one person over to You because of the way I react to someone who has hurt me? Amen.

Go

Luke 6:27-36 is a good passage about loving your enemies. Read it every day this wcck, and think about ways to love those who treat you badly. Praying for them is one way. Also read Proverbs 16:7.

✳ obeying Parents ✳

Think About This

It's really hard to obey my parents sometimes. I think they are treating me like a baby when they won't let me do something that everyone else gets to do. How can I obey them without being angry?

What God's Word Says

Children, obey your parents in everything, for this pleases the Lord. — Colossians 3:20

My Prayer Requests

_____

_____

_____

_____

_____

_____

God Works It Out

_____

_____

_____

Prayer

Father, I love my parents, but sometimes I think they are too strict. Although I don't mean to be disobedient, they treat me too much like a little child and I rebel. Help me to be obedient. Amen.

Go

The following scriptures tell how God wants us to treat our parents. Write them below as a reminder that God really wants you to obey your parents: Proverbs 10:17; Ephesians 6:1-2.

_____

_____

_____

_____

✳ Honoring Parents ✳

Think About This

Honoring my parents isn't easy when I'm not sure that they are living for You.

What God's Word Says

Honor your father and your mother, so that you may live long in the land the Lord your God is giving you.
— Exodus 20:12

My Prayer Requests

_____

_____

_____

_____

_____

God Works It Out

_____

_____

_____

Prayer

Lord, I know that honoring my parents is one of the Ten Commandments. Sometimes, though, I have trouble. You know my family's situation, and only You can help me deal with what bothers me about my parents. I will do Your will and honor my parents, no matter what the situation is. Amen.

Go

Look up the word "honor" in the dictionary. Then list below some ways that you should honor your parents. Also read these scriptures: Exodus 20:12 and Matthew 15:4.

_____

_____

_____

✳ Discipline ✳

Think About This

It's not easy to be corrected and punished for things I do wrong. I am embarassed and humiliated. I want to do and be right.

What God's Word Says

He who heeds discipline shows the way to life, but whoever ignores correction leads others astray.
                                        — Proverbs 10:17

A fool spurns his father's discipline, but whoever heeds correction shows prudence.   — Proverbs 15:5
("Prudence" is another word for wisdom.)

My Prayer Requests

_____

_____

_____

_____

_____

_____

God Works It Out

_____

_____

_____

Prayer

When I do something wrong, Lord, I know my parents are punishing me because I deserve it. Sometimes, though, it seems like I get into trouble for things I didn't do, or my punishment is unfair. Help me to honor You by honoring my parents' decision to discipline. Amen.

Go

Look up the words "discipline," "parents" and "children" in your Bible concordance or index. Then look up some more verses in the Bible to help you understand why God says it's good to have discipline. Write them below.

_____

_____

_____

✳ Living in Peace ✳

Think About This

Getting along with others—that's not an easy thing to do. Do You know, God, how hard it is to get along with my friends and family? Of course You do! You know everything!

What God's Word Says

All the believers were one in heart and mind.
— Acts 4:32

Make every effort to live in peace with all men and to be holy; without holiness no one will see the Lord. See to it that no one misses the grace of God and that no bitter root grows up to cause trouble and defile many.
— Hebrews 12:14-15

My Prayer Requests

_____

_____

_____

_____

_____

God Works It out

_____

_____

_____

Prayer

Father, I will try to get along with all those around me. It isn't always easy. I know You want me to allow Your love to show through in all I do, even in every day things like living at peace with others.

Go

Choose one person with whom you do not get along and then try to make your relationship better.

✳ Selfishness ✳

Think About This

Sometimes I just want to yell, "Me first!" How can I stop being so selfish even when I know it's wrong?

What God's Word Says

But many who are first will be last, and many who are last will be first. — Matthew 19:30

So in everything, do to others what you would have them do to you, for this sums up the Law and the Prophets. — Matthew 7:12 ("The Golden Rule")

My Prayer Requests

_____

_____

_____

_____

_____

God Works It Out

_____

_____

_____

Prayer

Help me to remember, Lord, that I shouldn't want to always be first. You want me to be an example for You and to put others before me. Let Your love and patience show through me each day. Amen.

Go

Memorize the Golden Rule—Matthew 7:12—and work on putting others first.

✳ Gossip ✳

Think About This

I am tempted to gossip about my friends. Sometimes I really hurt someone's feelings, but I don't know how to avoid gossiping. After all, everyone does it.

What God's Word Says

A gossip betrays a confidence, but a trustworthy man keeps a secret. — Proverbs 11:13

My Prayer Requests

_____

_____

_____

_____

_____

God Works It Out

_____

_____

_____

Prayer

Lord, I don't like it when someone talks about me. Let me remember that feeling when I am tempted to gossip about someone else. Even when a person is not my friend, or treats me badly, I do not have an excuse to gossip about him or her. Amen.

Go

There are lots of scriptures to help you remember that God doesn't want you to talk badly about others. Look up Proverbs 17:9, Proverbs 20:19, Leviticus 19:16 and Psalm 52:2.

✳ Judging Others ✳

Think About This

Do I have the right to judge others? After all, my friends really get themselves into some messes because they don't follow God's plan. Shouldn't I tell them how foolish they are?

What God's Word Says

Accept one another, then, just as Christ accepted you, in order to bring praise to God. — Romans 15:7

Do not judge, or you too will be judged. For in the same way you judge others, you will be judged, and with the measure you use, it will be measured to you. — Matthew 7:1-2

My Prayer Requests

_____

_____

_____

_____

_____

_____

God Works It Out

_____

_____

_____

Prayer

Help me not to judge anyone else, Lord. Matthew 7:1-6 tells the story about the speck and the log. Help me not to tell a friend about a little speck of sin in his or her life when I have a big log of sin in mine. Amen.

Go

Draw a cartoon below of the story of the speck and the log, and let it remind you of how silly it is to tell people about problems they have when you have some really big problems of your own.

✳ Forgiving ✳

Think About This

I have a hard time forgiving others. I think I am always right—it's always someone else's fault that we had a fight or my feelings got hurt. But I know in my heart that I can't always be right.

What God's Word Says

Be kind and compassionate to one another, forgiving each other, just as in Christ God forgave you.
— Ephesians 4:32

My Prayer Requests

_____

_____

_____

_____

_____

_____

God Works It Out

_____

_____

_____

Prayer

Forgiving someone is hard to do, Father. When someone has done something to hurt me or make me angry, I have a hard time acting like it didn't happen. Help me to forgive others just as You have forgiven me. Amen.

Go

Look up the words "forgive" and "compassion" in a dictionary. Then look up both words in the Bible concordance and find some verses about forgiveness to write below and memorize.

_____

_____

_____

_____

✳ Praying for others ✳

Think About This

I will pray for others. It's awesome to think that my little prayer can hold so much power that someone will become well or will learn about You. Thank You, Lord, for putting this power behind my prayer. You are really awesome.

What God's Word Says

And the prayer offered in faith will make the sick person well; the Lord will raise him up. If he has sinned, he will be forgiven. Therefore...pray for each other. The prayer of a righteous man is powerful and effective.
— James 5:15-16

My Prayer Requests

_____

_____

_____

_____

_____

God Works It Out

_____

_____

_____

Prayer

There are lots of people around me who need You, Lord. Help me to remember to pray for them. Amen.

Go

Pray for at least one other person each day this week. Make a card or write a note to tell someone you are praying for him or her.

✳ Loving others ✳

Think About This

You want us to love one another, Lord. It's not easy to do. Some homeless people look scary to me. The neighbor down the block yells at me for no reason. I have a teacher who just doesn't seem to like me.

What God's Word Says

This is the message you heard from the beginning: "We should love one another." — 1 John 3:11

And the second [greatest commandment] is like it: "Love your neighbor as yourself." — Matthew 22:39

My Prayer Requests

_____

_____

_____

_____

_____

_____

God Works It Out

_____

_____

_____

Prayer

Father, remind me that You want me to love others as much as I love myself. That may mean that I have to be nice to someone who really makes me angry. Help me to remember that I am not always easy to love, either.

Go

Reach out to someone who needs to know about God's love. Bake cookies for your teacher, fix a small child's toy or volunteer to help at a shelter.

✳

✳ What I Learned ✳

✳ In this Chapter, I learned:

_____

_____

_____

✳ My favorite Bible verse in this Chapter is:

_____

_____

✳ I was surprised to find out that:

_____

_____

_____

✳

✳ I discovered this about myself:

_____

_____

_____

✳ I discovered this about God:

_____

_____

_____

✳ How I plan to act on what I've learned:

_____

_____

_____

This Thing Called Life

They're all around you: Problems! They discourage you and make you feel hopeless. Temptations try to make you sin and feel worthless.

Sometimes you do something to disappoint those who love you. There are times when someone you love disappoints you.

But just when you feel that you can't count on anyone or can't do anything right yourself, God lets you know that He is in control. You realize that God always loves you and He will help you to do what's right. He will also take those disappointments that others cause you and help you to be forgiving and loving.

God is waiting to hear your disappointments and hurts. He is willing and ready to help you forgive others, just as He forgives you.

Thank God that He is so loving and merciful!

✳ forgiven ✳

Think About This

I know I am a sinner. It makes me feel bad that I disappoint You, God. But thank You for forgiving me again and again.

What God's Word Says

While we were still sinners, Christ died for us.
— Romans 5:8

There is rejoicing in the presence of the angels of God over one sinner who repents. — Luke 15:10

My Prayer Requests

_____

_____

_____

_____

_____

_____

God Works It Out

_____

_____

_____

Prayer

Forgive me, Lord, when I sin. Help me to remember that Jesus gave His life because of my sins. Amen.

Go

Read and memorize Matthew 18:14. When you sin, think about Jesus on the cross. He died just for you. Pray for forgiveness and try to do better.

✳ Drugs and Alcohol ✳

Think About This

Drugs and alcohol are all around me. I need God's strength to keep from getting involved in these things that I know are harmful to me.

What God's Word Says

Watch and pray so that you will not fall into temptation. The spirit is willing, but the body is weak.
— Matthew 26:41

My Prayer Requests

_____

_____

_____

_____

_____

God Works It out

_____

_____

_____

Prayer

Lord, so many of my friends are trying drugs or drinking alcohol—even some of my friends who go to church. How can I stay away from these things when they are all around me? Help me, Lord. Amen.

Go

Memorize Psalm 34:14. If alcohol or drugs are offered to you, talk to your parents or pastor. Pray that God will help you to not be tempted. Remember: your body is His property, so take good care of it.

✻ Peer Pressure ✻

Think About This

My friend (or brother or sister) is trying to get me to do wrong things. I know in my heart that these things are not God's will, but it is hard to say "no " when someone else is pressuring me so much.

What God's Word Says

No temptation has seized you except what is common to man. And God is faithful; he will not let you be tempted beyond what you can bear. But when you are tempted, he will also provide a way out so that you can stand up under it. — 1 Corinthians 10:13

My Prayer Requests

_____

_____

_____

_____

_____

God Works It Out

_____

_____

_____

Prayer

Thank You, Lord, for understanding that temptations will sometimes get the better of me. It is hard
to resist doing something wrong, and people push
hard at me to get me to do wrong things. Thank
You for 1 Corinthians 10:13, so that I know You are
there always to help me do what is right. Amen.

Go

Memorize 1 Corinthians 10:13 and Acts 5:29.

✳ Heroes ✳

Think About This

My hero (a movie or music star, sports player or family member) was caught committing a crime. I am crushed to think that my hero could do such a thing. How can I ever forgive this person? Who will I look up to now? Can I trust anyone?

What God's Word Says

Do not imitate what is evil but what is good. Anyone who does what is good is from God. Anyone who does what is evil has not seen God. — 3 John 11

Do not put your trust in princes, in mortal men, who cannot save. When their spirit departs, they return to the ground; on that very day their plans come to nothing. — Psalm 146:3-4

My Prayer Requests

_____

_____

_____

_____

_____

God Works It Out

_____

_____

_____

Prayer

Lord, my hero has gotten in trouble. I looked up to this person. I thought that he (or she) was perfect. I wanted to be like him (or her). Now I am disappointed. Thank You for Jesus, who set a perfect example for me and is the only real hero. Amen.

Go

List all of your heroes. Then list some people from the Bible whom you admire. Besides Jesus, no one is perfect (even godly heroes, although they can serve as encouragement). Remember to pattern your life most carefully after Jesus, not after worldly models.

My Heroes   **Bible Heroes**

_____   _____

_____   _____

_____   _____

✳ Avoiding Sin ✳

Think About This

Doing right seems to be harder each day in a world full of sin. I want to do only that with which God would be pleased.

What God's Word Says

Even a child is known by his actions, by whether his conduct is pure and right. — Proverbs 20:11

If you do what is right, will you not be accepted? But if you do not do what is right, sin is crouching at your door, it desires to have you, but you must master it. — Genesis 4:7

My Prayer Requests

_____

_____

_____

_____

_____

God Works It Out

_____

_____

_____

Prayer

Sin is lurking at my door, God. Help me to hang on to what is good and right in Your eyes. Amen.

Go

Memorize this part of today's scripture: "Sin is crouching at your door; it desires to have you, but you must master it."

✳ Answers to Prayer ✳

Think About This

I have asked God to help me with something, but I don't think He has answered me yet. How do I know when God has answered my prayer?

What God's Word Says

Wait for the Lord; be strong and take heart and wait for the Lord. — Psalm 27:14

The joy of the Lord is your strength. — Nehemiah 8:10

My Prayer Requests

_____

_____

_____

_____

_____

_____

God Works It out

_____

_____

_____

Prayer

I feel like my prayers aren't being answered, Lord. Help me to hang on and do the best I can while You are working out my problem. Amen.

Go

Memorize the two scriptures at left to help you remember that God is working out your problems.

✳ What I Learned ✳

✳ In this chapter, I learned:

_____

_____

_____

✳ My favorite Bible verse in this chapter is:

_____

_____

✳ I was surprised to find out that:

_____

_____

_____

✳ I discovered this about myself:

_____

_____

_____

✳ I discovered this about God:

_____

_____

_____

✳ How I plan to act on what I've learned:

_____

_____

_____

Praising God

Sometimes we just feel like praising God! Praise can come in the form of a quiet thought, a song, or even a great big shout. You might write a poem to God or write down a special prayer to read to God over and over.

All of these ways of praising God are a form of prayer. And God really loves that. He loves to hear you say, sing or shout praises to Him. He loves even the tiniest whisper of praise.

God especially loves your praise when you share it with others. You can join your family in praise and worship at home or at church. Or you can share in praise and prayer with a friend.

Sometimes you have the opportunity to praise God in front of someone who doesn't know much about Him. What a wonderful way to introduce others to our great and awesome God! Remember to praise God often.

✳ Praise Him! ✳

Think About This

I feel like praising You, Lord. It makes me feel so good to just shout out praises to You.

What God's Word Says

Let everything that has breath praise the Lord.
— Psalm 150:6

My Prayer Requests

_____

_____

_____

_____

_____

_____

_____

God Works It Out

_____

_____

_____

Prayer

I love You, Lord. Sometimes I feel like telling You
how wonderful You are. Thank You! Amen.

Go

Read Psalm 103. Write a praise poem to God below.

_____

_____

_____

_____

_____

✳ Sing Praises ✳

Think About This

I will sing praises to You, Lord. When I feel sad, I will sing praises to You. When I feel glad, I will also sing praises to You.

What God's Word Says

Praise the Lord. Praise the Lord, O my soul. I will praise the Lord all my life; I will sing praise to my God as long as I live. — Psalm 146:1-2

I will sing and make music to the Lord. — Psalm 27:6

My Prayer Requests

_____

_____

_____

_____

_____

_____

God Works It Out

_____

_____

_____

Prayer

I love to sing praises to You, God. All my troubles seem to disappear when I am praising You. Amen.

Go

Write a song to God this week. If you play an instrument, use it to play the song. If not, sing or hum a new tune. Teach it to your friends!

✳ Praise in Worship ✳

Think About This

I will worship You, Lord. Praising You is a form of worship. I love to praise and worship You.

What God's Word Says

Shout for joy to the Lord, all the earth. Worship the Lord with gladness; come before him with joyful songs. Know that the Lord is God. It is he who made us, and we are his; we are his people, the sheep of his pasture. Enter his gates with thanksgiving and his courts with praise; give thanks to him and praise his name. For the Lord is good and his love endures forever; his faithfulness continues through all generations.

— Psalm 100

My Prayer Requests

_____

_____

_____

_____

_____

God Works It Out

_____

_____

_____

Prayer

I shout for joy when I think of how wonderful and magnificent You are, heavenly Father. You are worthy of my praise and the praise of everyone on the earth that You created. Amen.

Go

Think of ten things for which to praise God. Write them below.

1. _____   6. _____

2. _____   7. _____

3. _____   8. _____

4. _____   9. _____

5. _____   10. _____

✶ Witness of Praise ✶

Think About This

I will praise You to others, Lord. My friends need to know how much You love them. They will learn of Your great love through my praises to You.

What God's Word Says

My mouth will speak in praise of the Lord. Let every creature praise his holy name for ever and ever.
— Psalm 145:21

My Prayer Requests

_____

_____

_____

_____

_____

God Works It Out

_____

_____

_____

Prayer

I praise You and thank You, Father. I will tell others
about Your greatness and of Your great love for each
of us. Amen.

Go

Tell two or more people about the Lord and what
He has done for you.

✻ Loving God ✻

Think About This

I love you, Lord. It makes me feel special to know that You love me, too.

What God's Word Says

Love the Lord your God with all your heart and with all your soul and with all your mind and with all your strength. — Mark 12:30

Love the Lord your God with all your heart and with all your soul and with all your strength. — Deuteronomy 6:5

And this is love: that we walk in obedience to his commands. — 2 John 6

My Prayer Requests

_____

_____

_____

_____

_____

God Works It Out

_____

_____

_____

Prayer

I love You, Lord, and will try each day to love You more and more. The ways I can show how much I love You are by obeying Your Word, serving You and telling others about You. Amen.

Go

I will tell You everyday how much I love You, Lord. I will also tell someone else about you.

✳ What I Learned ✳

✳ In this chapter, I learned:

_____

_____

_____

✳ My favorite Bible verse in this chapter is:

_____

_____

✳ I was surprised to find out that:

_____

_____

_____

✳ **I discovered this about myself:**

_____

_____

_____

✳ **I discovered this about God:**

_____

_____

_____

✳ **How I plan to act on what I've learned:**

_____

_____

_____

Uncontrollable Monsters!

Everyone has feelings. Sometimes they are good, but sometimes you have bad feelings. At times, you might sense that your feelings are out of control.

How can you keep your feelings under control? How can you push bad feelings aside and continue to serve God?

With God, everything can be in control. With prayer you can have God's help to keep your feelings, temper, fears, and jealousies under control. If you talk to God as soon as any of these feelings creep up on you, you will be in better control of your feelings.

Thank God for helping you to control your feelings when they seem to be uncontrollable monsters.

✳ Discouragement ✳

Think About This

When things don't go how I'd like, I get discouraged and disappointed. It's hard to live for God when these feelings of disappointment get in the way.

What God's Word Says

Do not be discouraged, for the Lord your God will be with you wherever you go. — Joshua 1:9

My Prayer Requests

_____

_____

_____

_____

_____

God Works It Out

_____

_____

_____

Prayer

Lord, I didn't make the ball team (or the cheerleading squad, the play, etc.). It is so embarrassing to be one of the few not chosen, or to be the last one chosen. Help me to remember that what happens to me is in Your perfect plan for my life. Amen.

Go

Write below some disappointments that you have experienced. Then write down some ways that God worked out these situations. Remind yourself that God loves you and works things out for your good. Use Romans 8:31 as your special verse this week.

_____

_____

_____

✴ Am I Worthless? ✴

Think About This

I can't do anything right. Some days, I'd just like to crawl into a big hole and pull the ground in over me. Why is it that I seem to mess things up all of the time?

What God's Word Says

For we are God's workmanship, created in Christ Jesus to do good works, which God prepared in advance for us to do. — Ephesians 2:10

My Prayer Requests

_____

_____

_____

_____

_____

God Works It Out

_____

_____

_____

Prayer

When I don't seem to be able to do anything right, help me remember that I am special to You. Amen.

Go

Write out Matthew 18:3-4 and 19:14 below. When you feel bad about yourself, imagine that you are one of the children that Jesus took upon His lap. He loves you, just as you are.

_____

_____

_____

_____

✳ Not Alone ✳

Think About This

Sometimes I need to feel You beside me, so I know I am not alone. Thank You for being there, Lord.

What God's Word Says

"For I am with you," declares the Lord Almighty. "And my Spirit remains among you. Do not fear."
— Haggai 2:4-5

My Prayer Requests

_____

_____

_____

_____

_____

God Works It Out

_____

_____

_____

Prayer

When I feel alone, Lord, I will remember that You work out everything for my good, even though I don't always see the good right away. You are with me always. Thank You. Amen.

Go

Read back over your prayer journal and look at all of the prayer requests that you have written down in the past days. Then read the "God Works It Out" sections. See how God has worked in your life!

✳ Worries ✳

Think About This

I get so worried about things in my life, Lord, and I don't know how to handle these worries.

What God's Word Says

Come to me, all you who are weary and burdened, and I will give you rest. — Matthew 11:28

Cast all your anxiety on him because he cares for you. — 1 Peter 5:7

My Prayer Requests

_____

_____

_____

_____

_____

God Works It Out

_____

_____

_____

Prayer

I am so worried, Lord. Schoolwork, friend problems, a loved one who is ill…how can I keep from feeling so burdened with these worries? Please send me Your comfort and guidance. Amen.

Go

Read Luke 12:22-34 every day this week. God wants you to give your worries to Him and live a joyful life. God is able to take care of any need you have.

✳ Jealousy ✳

Think About This

Sometimes I get so jealous of others. I have trouble being joyful when a friend wins a game over me, or if someone gets something that I really want.

What God's Word Says

But if you harbor bitter envy and selfish ambition in your hearts, do not boast about it or deny the truth. Such "wisdom" does not come down from heaven but is earthly, unspiritual, of the devil. For where you have envy and selfish ambition, there you find disorder and every evil practice. But the wisdom that comes from heaven is first of all pure; then peace-loving, considerate, submissive, full of mercy and good fruit, impartial and sincere. Peacemakers who sow in peace raise a harvest of righteousness. — James 3:14-18

My Prayer Requests

_____

_____

_____

_____

_____

God Works It Out

_____

_____

_____

Prayer

Lord, help me to remember that You want me to live in peace with others, and jealousy will stop me from doing that. In Galatians 5:26 You tell us to not provoke and envy each other. I will try to not be jealous of others. Amen.

Go

Notice when you are jealous of someone. Then think about what you have that that person does not have. Remember that God has given you everything that you need. Memorize Proverbs 27:4.

✳ Anger ✳

Think About This

Sometimes a person can push at me for a long time before I lose my temper. Other times, I can get angry very easily, although I don't mean to.

What God's Word Says

In your anger do not sin. Do not let the sun go down while you are still angry. — Ephesians 4:26

My Prayer Requests

_____

_____

_____

_____

_____

_____

God Works It Out

_____

_____

_____

Prayer

I know You don't want me to get angry. Proverbs has a lot of verses about being "quick-tempered." I will read them and try to control my temper. Amen.

Go

Read these proverbs and find a good one to memorize—these verses will help you to control your temper: Proverbs 15:18; 21:19; 22:24; 25:21; and 29:22.

✳ Joy of Prayer ✳

Think About This

I feel better when I pray, God. You can work anything out for me, and I know I can lay all my problems, worries and fears at Your feet.

What God's Word Says

Is any one of you in trouble? He should pray. Is anyone happy? Let him sing songs of praise.   — James 5:13

My Prayer Requests

_____

_____

_____

_____

_____

God Works It out

_____

_____

_____

Prayer

Dear Father, it is great knowing that You love me
and want to be part of my life each day. I pray for
all my family and friends, that they will find joy in
having a personal prayer life, too. Amen.

Go

Make a list below of times when you like to pray.

_____

_____

_____

_____

✳ What I Learned ✳

✳ In this chapter, I learned:

_____

_____

_____

✳ My favorite Bible verse in this chapter is:

_____

_____

✳ I was surprised to find out that:

_____

_____

_____

✳ I discovered this about myself:

_____

_____

_____

✳ I discovered this about God:

_____

_____

_____

✳ How I plan to act on what I've learned:

_____

_____

_____

A Gratitude Attitude

Don't you hate it when you do something really special for people and they don't even notice? Those two little words—"thank you"—can make a big difference, can't they? You naturally want to do more for a person who takes the time to notice the good things you do. It's also nice to hear "you did a good job."

God loves to hear your thanks, too. He has done so much for you! You are a wonderful creation in God's own image. You count on God to help you in your life each day.

God has also given us the greatest gift of all: eternal life through Jesus Christ. How can you keep from giving God your thanks for that wonderful act?

✳ for Salvation ✳

Think About This

Jesus gave His life willingly, so that I can live in heaven. What love He must have for me! Thank You, Jesus.

What God's Word Says

I lay down my life—only to take it up again. No one takes it from me, but I lay it down of my own accord. I have authority to lay it down and authority to take it up again. — John 10:17-18

My Prayer Requests

_____

_____

_____

_____

_____

_____

God Works It Out

Prayer

Jesus gave His life willingly. Help me to keep that thought in my mind. When things get tough, when I sin or when I feel unloved, let that thought come to me. Thank You for all You have done for me. Thank You most of all for Jesus. Amen.

Go

Each day this week, tell someone about Jesus' love, or pray for someone to come to know Jesus.

✴ For Jesus ✴

Think About This

I thank God for sending His Son to be our Savior. God must really love me to do that.

What God's Word Says

She will give birth to a son, and you are to give him the name Jesus, because he will save his people from their sins. — Matthew 1:21

My Prayer Requests

_____

_____

_____

_____

_____

_____

God Works It Out

_____

_____

_____

Prayer

Father, thank You for sending Jesus to earth as Your Son to save us all from our sins. I know that You must really love me. Amen.

Go

Read about Jesus' miracle birth in the books of Matthew and Luke in the Bible.

✳ For God's Promises ✳

Think About This

Jesus is a promise fulfilled by God. Thank You for keeping Your promise of a Savior, Lord.

What God's Word Says

For to us a child is born, to us a son is given, and the government will be on his shoulders. And he will be called Wonderful Counselor, Mighty God, Everlasting Father, Prince of Peace. — Isaiah 9:6

My Prayer Requests

_____

_____

_____

_____

_____

_____

God Works It out

_____

_____

_____

Prayer

Thank You for a loving Savior. I see in the Bible
how You kept Your promises to Your children. I
know You will keep Your promises to me, too. Amen.

Go

Read Isaiah 9:1-7 to find out what God has prom-
ised His people.

✳ For Making Me Special ✳

Think About This

God made me special and He wants His best for me. How can I thank Him? The best way for me to thank God is to love Him and obey Him.

What God's Word Says

Your hands made me and formed me.
— Psalm 119:73

And we know that in all things God works for the good of those who love him. — Romans 8:28

My Prayer Requests

_____

_____

_____

_____

_____

_____

God Works It Out

_____

_____

_____

Prayer

Thank You for making me special, Lord. When things are going wrong, I will remember that You made me special and that You love me. Amen.

Go

Every day, thank God for making you a special person, and remind yourself that He has a purpose for you. Write down below some of the things you think will happen to you according to God's plan.

_____

_____

_____

✳ For God's Love ✳

Think About This

God loves me. I will remember that whenever I feel unloved. My God loves me more than anyone else in this whole world loves me.

What God's Word Says

And so we know and rely on the love God has for us. God is love. Whoever lives in love lives in God, and God in him. — 1 John 4:16

My Prayer Requests

_____

_____

_____

_____

_____

God Works It Out

_____

_____

_____

Prayer

Thank You for loving me, God. Sometimes I feel like no one loves me. But I can remember that You always do. You're never too busy for me. Amen.

Go

Each day, spend time thinking about how much God loves you. Read these scriptures: Jeremiah 31:3; John 3:16; John 16:27; 1 John 4:10; and 1 John 4:19.

✶ What I Learned ✶

✶ In this chapter, I learned:

_____

_____

_____

✶ My favorite Bible verse in this chapter is:

_____

_____

✶ I was surprised to find out that:

_____

_____

_____

✳ **I discovered this about myself:**

_____

_____

_____

✳ **I discovered this about God:**

_____

_____

_____

✳ **How I plan to act on what I've learned:**

_____

_____

_____

In Conclusion

* I completed my Prayer Journal on:

_____

* The most important thing I learned was:

_____

_____

* My most important answer to prayer was:

_____

_____

_____

* I will continue to pray for:

_____

_____